Vietnam

Everything You Need to Know

Copyright © 2024 by Noah Gil-Smith.

All rights reserved. No part of this book may be reproduced, distributed, or transmitted in any form or by any means, including photocopying, recording, or other electronic or mechanical methods, without the prior written permission of the publisher, except in the case of brief quotations embodied in critical reviews and certain other noncommercial uses permitted by copyright law. This book was created with the assistance of Artificial Intelligence. The content presented in this book is for entertainment purposes only. It should not be considered as a substitute for professional advice or comprehensive research. Readers are encouraged to independently verify any information and consult relevant experts for specific matters. The author and publisher disclaim any liability or responsibility for any loss, injury, or inconvenience caused or alleged to be caused directly or indirectly by the information presented in this book.

Introduction to Vietnam 6

A Brief History: From Ancient Dynasties to Modern Times 8

Colonial Vietnam: Influence and Legacy 11

Vietnam War: Understanding its Impact 14

Modern Vietnam: Economic Growth and Development 17

Geography and Climate: Diverse Landscapes and Weather Patterns 20

Flora and Fauna: Exploring Vietnam's Biodiversity 22

Vietnamese Cuisine: A Culinary Adventure 24

Must-Try Dishes: From Pho to Banh Mi 27

Traditional Ingredients and Cooking Techniques 29

Street Food Culture: Where to Find the Best Eats 31

Iconic Sights: Exploring Vietnam's Top Tourist Attractions 33

Ha Long Bay: A Natural Wonder 36

Ho Chi Minh City (Saigon): A Vibrant Metropolis 38

Hanoi: Capital City Rich in History 40

Hue: Imperial City and Cultural Heartland 42

Hoi An: Ancient Town of Lanterns and Traditions 44

Da Nang: Gateway to Central Vietnam 47

Nha Trang: Beach Paradise and Water Activities 49

Mekong Delta: Exploring Vietnam's Rice Bowl 52

Vietnamese Traditions and Customs: Etiquette and Social Norms 54

Festivals and Celebrations: Colorful Cultural Experiences 57

Vietnamese Art and Architecture: Beauty in Design 59

Traditional Music and Performing Arts 61

Religious Diversity: Buddhism, Confucianism, and more 63

Ethnic Minorities: Rich Tapestry of Cultures 66

Vietnamese Language: Basics and Common Phrases 69

Language Variation Across Regions 71

Vietnamese Writing System: Characters and Alphabet 74

Learning Vietnamese: Tips for Language Acquisition 76

Daily Life in Vietnam: Urban vs. Rural 79

Transportation: Navigating Vietnam's Roads and Waterways 82

Education and Healthcare: Access and Challenges 85

Economy and Industry: Growth Sectors and Challenges 87

Social Issues: Poverty, Corruption, and Environmental Concerns 90

Tourism Trends: Sustainable Travel in Vietnam 92

Adventure Tourism: Trekking, Cycling, and Water Sports 95

Vietnam's Role in Southeast Asia: Politics and Diplomacy 98

International Relations: Vietnam's Global Partnerships 100

Vietnamese Diaspora: Communities 102

Future Outlook: Opportunities and Challenges 105

Epilogue 108

Introduction to Vietnam

Nestled in the heart of Southeast Asia, Vietnam captivates with its rich history, diverse culture, and stunning landscapes. From bustling cities to serene countryside, this dynamic country offers a tapestry of experiences waiting to be explored.

Vietnam is bordered by China to the north, Laos to the northwest, Cambodia to the southwest, and the South China Sea to the east. Its strategic location has shaped its history, as it served as a crossroads for trade and cultural exchange for centuries.

The country's history is a complex tapestry woven with threads of triumph and turmoil. Ancient dynasties ruled over this land, leaving behind a legacy of art, architecture, and philosophy. In more recent times, Vietnam endured centuries of foreign rule, including Chinese domination and French colonialism.

However, perhaps no period in Vietnam's history is as well-known or as impactful as the Vietnam War. This conflict, which raged from 1955 to 1975, pitted the communist forces of North Vietnam against the anti-communist forces of South Vietnam and its allies, including the United States. The war left a profound mark on the country and its people, shaping its political landscape and social fabric for generations to come.

Despite its tumultuous past, Vietnam has emerged as a vibrant and resilient nation in the modern era. Since the end of the Vietnam War, the country has undergone rapid economic growth and development, transforming itself into one of the fastest-growing economies in Southeast Asia. Today, Vietnam is known for its bustling cities, thriving industries, and welcoming people.

Geographically, Vietnam boasts a diverse landscape that ranges from lush rice paddies and winding rivers to rugged mountains and pristine beaches. Its climate varies from tropical in the south to subtropical in the north, offering visitors a range of environments to explore throughout the year.

Culturally, Vietnam is a melting pot of ethnicities, languages, and traditions. From the bustling markets of Ho Chi Minh City to the ancient temples of Hanoi, the country's rich heritage is on display at every turn. Traditional customs and values continue to play a central role in Vietnamese society, shaping everything from family life to business practices.

In this book, we will delve deeper into the many facets of Vietnam, exploring its history, culture, cuisine, and more. Whether you're a seasoned traveler or a curious armchair explorer, join us on a journey through this fascinating country as we uncover everything you need to know about Vietnam.

A Brief History: From Ancient Dynasties to Modern Times

Vietnam's history is a tapestry woven with threads of ancient dynasties, colonial rule, and revolutionary struggle. From its earliest days to the present, the country has been shaped by a diverse array of influences, leaving behind a rich legacy that continues to resonate today.

The story of Vietnam begins thousands of years ago, with the rise of the ancient kingdom of Van Lang in the Red River Delta. This early civilization laid the foundation for what would later become the Vietnamese nation, establishing a culture based on agriculture, bronze casting, and social hierarchy.

Over the centuries, Vietnam experienced waves of migration and conquest, as various peoples from neighboring regions settled in the fertile lands of the Red River Delta. By the 3rd century BCE, the kingdom of Au Lac had emerged as a dominant power in the region, ruling over much of present-day northern Vietnam.

In 111 BCE, Vietnam came under the control of the Han Dynasty of China, marking the beginning of centuries of Chinese domination. Despite periods of resistance and rebellion, Vietnam remained under Chinese rule for over a millennium, during which time it adopted many elements of Chinese culture, including Confucianism, Buddhism, and the Chinese writing system.

In the 10th century CE, Vietnam gained its independence from China under the leadership of the legendary hero, Ngo Quyen. This marked the beginning of the period known as the Early Le Dynasty, during which Vietnam experienced a cultural and political renaissance. The Ly and Tran Dynasties that followed saw the flourishing of Vietnamese art, literature, and philosophy, as well as the expansion of the country's territory southward.

However, Vietnam's independence was once again threatened in the 19th century, as European powers began to encroach on Southeast Asia. In 1858, France invaded Vietnam, establishing colonial rule over the entire country by 1884. Under French control, Vietnam was subjected to exploitation and oppression, leading to widespread resistance and rebellion.

The 20th century brought further upheaval to Vietnam, as the country became embroiled in wars of independence against first the French and then the United States. The First Indochina War, which lasted from 1946 to 1954, resulted in the defeat of the French colonial forces and the partitioning of Vietnam into the communist North and the anti-communist South.

The Vietnam War, which followed in the 1960s and 1970s, was a protracted and bloody conflict that pitted the communist forces of North Vietnam, supported by the Soviet Union and China, against the anti-communist forces of South Vietnam, backed by the United States and its allies. The war ended in 1975 with the fall of Saigon and the reunification of Vietnam under communist rule.

Since the end of the Vietnam War, the country has undergone rapid economic growth and development, emerging as one of the fastest-growing economies in Southeast Asia. Today, Vietnam is a thriving nation with a rich cultural heritage and a dynamic population that looks towards the future while honoring its past.

Colonial Vietnam: Influence and Legacy

Colonial Vietnam stands as a pivotal period in the nation's history, marked by foreign influence and lasting legacies that continue to shape the country to this day. The era of colonialism in Vietnam began in the mid-19th century when France, seeking to expand its empire in Southeast Asia, established a foothold in the region.

In 1858, French forces launched a military campaign against Vietnam, known as the Cochinchina Campaign, seizing control of the southern region of the country. This marked the beginning of French colonial rule, which would eventually extend to encompass the entire territory of Vietnam by 1884.

Under French rule, Vietnam was subjected to profound changes in its political, economic, and social structures. The French implemented a system of direct colonial administration, appointing French officials to govern the country and imposing French laws and institutions.

Economically, Vietnam was exploited for its resources, with French colonial authorities extracting natural wealth such as rice, rubber, and coal to benefit the French economy. Large plantations were established, and Vietnamese peasants were forced to work as laborers under harsh conditions.

Socially, the French introduced Western education and modern infrastructure to Vietnam, but these benefits were largely reserved for the French and Vietnamese elites. The majority of the population remained impoverished and marginalized, leading to widespread discontent and resistance.

Culturally, French colonialism had a profound impact on Vietnamese society, influencing everything from language and cuisine to art and architecture. French became the language of administration and education, leading to a gradual decline in the use of Vietnamese in official contexts.

Architecturally, French colonial influence is evident in the grand boulevards, ornate buildings, and colonial villas that still dot the landscape of cities like Hanoi and Ho Chi Minh City. French cuisine also left its mark on Vietnamese culinary traditions, with dishes like banh mi (French bread sandwich) and cafe sua da (Vietnamese iced coffee) becoming beloved staples of Vietnamese cuisine.

Despite the changes brought about by French colonialism, resistance to foreign rule remained strong throughout Vietnam. From the early days of French occupation, Vietnamese patriots such as Phan Boi Chau and Nguyen Ai Quoc (later known as Ho Chi Minh) organized movements aimed at achieving independence and sovereignty for Vietnam.

The legacy of colonialism in Vietnam is complex and multifaceted, with both positive and negative aspects. While French colonial rule brought modernization and development to Vietnam, it also led to exploitation, inequality, and the loss of national sovereignty. Today, Vietnam continues to grapple with the lasting effects of its colonial past as it navigates the challenges of the modern world.

Vietnam War: Understanding its Impact

The Vietnam War stands as one of the most significant conflicts of the 20th century, leaving a profound impact on Vietnam and the world at large. Lasting from 1955 to 1975, the war was a complex and divisive conflict that pitted the communist forces of North Vietnam, supported by the Soviet Union and China, against the anti-communist forces of South Vietnam, backed by the United States and its allies.

Rooted in the struggle for Vietnamese independence and reunification, the Vietnam War was fueled by Cold War tensions and the broader geopolitical rivalry between the United States and the Soviet Union. The conflict escalated in the 1960s as the United States became increasingly involved, deploying hundreds of thousands of troops to support the South Vietnamese government in its fight against the communist insurgency.

The Vietnam War was characterized by its brutality and intensity, with both sides engaging in guerrilla warfare, bombings, and atrocities that exacted a heavy toll on the civilian population. The use of chemical weapons, such as Agent Orange, by the United States further contributed to the devastation, leaving a lasting legacy of environmental and health issues for generations of Vietnamese.

The war also had profound social and political consequences, both in Vietnam and the United States. In Vietnam, the conflict resulted in the loss of millions of lives and the displacement of countless families, leaving deep scars on the nation's psyche. The reunification of Vietnam under communist rule in 1975 marked a turning point in the country's history, but it also ushered in a period of hardship and reconstruction as Vietnam sought to rebuild in the aftermath of war.

In the United States, the Vietnam War sparked widespread protests and social unrest, as many Americans questioned the morality and legality of the war effort. The anti-war movement gained momentum throughout the 1960s and 1970s, culminating in large-scale demonstrations, draft resistance, and acts of civil disobedience. The war also strained relations between the government and the American public, leading to a crisis of confidence in political institutions and authority.

The legacy of the Vietnam War continues to reverberate today, shaping the political, social, and cultural landscape of both Vietnam and the United States. In Vietnam, the war is remembered as a heroic struggle for independence and reunification, while in the United States, it remains a divisive and contentious chapter in American history.

Despite the passage of time, the wounds of war have yet to fully heal, and the Vietnam War continues to serve as a reminder of the human cost of conflict and the importance of striving for peace and reconciliation. Understanding the impact of the Vietnam War is essential for grasping the complexities of modern Vietnam and the enduring legacy of one of the most consequential conflicts of the 20th century.

Modern Vietnam: Economic Growth and Development

Modern Vietnam is a story of resilience, transformation, and rapid economic growth. Since the end of the Vietnam War in 1975, the country has undergone remarkable changes, emerging as one of the fastest-growing economies in Southeast Asia. Central to Vietnam's economic success has been its transition from a centrally planned economy to a socialist-oriented market economy, a process known as "Doi Moi," initiated in 1986.

Under the Doi Moi reforms, Vietnam embraced market-oriented policies and opened its doors to foreign investment and trade. This shift unleashed a wave of entrepreneurial energy and innovation, propelling Vietnam onto the global stage as a dynamic and competitive economy. Today, Vietnam is recognized as one of the most attractive destinations for foreign direct investment in the region.

The Vietnamese government has pursued a strategy of export-led growth, focusing on key industries such as manufacturing, electronics, textiles, and agriculture. Foreign investment has poured into Vietnam's industrial zones, fueling the expansion of factories and production facilities across the country. Vietnam's accession to the World Trade Organization (WTO) in 2007 further bolstered its integration into the global economy, opening up new opportunities for trade and investment.

One of the driving forces behind Vietnam's economic success has been its young and dynamic workforce. With a median age of just 30 years old, Vietnam boasts a large and rapidly growing labor force that is highly skilled and adaptable. This demographic dividend has attracted multinational corporations seeking to tap into Vietnam's abundant human capital and low-cost manufacturing base.

In addition to its thriving industrial sector, Vietnam has also seen significant growth in services, particularly tourism and information technology. The country's picturesque landscapes, rich cultural heritage, and affordable cost of living have made it a popular destination for travelers from around the world. Meanwhile, Vietnam's burgeoning IT sector has earned it a reputation as a regional hub for software development and outsourcing.

Despite its impressive economic achievements, Vietnam still faces a number of challenges on the road to further development. Income inequality remains a persistent issue, with disparities between urban and rural areas and different regions of the country. Moreover, Vietnam is vulnerable to external shocks, such as fluctuations in global commodity prices and geopolitical tensions in the region.

Nevertheless, Vietnam's trajectory of economic growth and development shows no signs of slowing down. With a young and dynamic population, a strategic location in Southeast Asia, and a commitment to reform and innovation, Vietnam is poised to continue its ascent as a key player in the global economy. As the country navigates the opportunities and challenges of the 21st century, the story of modern Vietnam is one of optimism, resilience, and endless potential.

Geography and Climate: Diverse Landscapes and Weather Patterns

Vietnam's geography is as diverse as it is breathtaking, offering a wide range of landscapes that captivate the senses and inspire wonder. Situated in Southeast Asia, Vietnam is bordered by China to the north, Laos to the northwest, Cambodia to the southwest, and the South China Sea to the east. This strategic location not only shapes Vietnam's cultural identity but also influences its climate and natural features.

From the towering peaks of the northern highlands to the lush deltas of the Mekong in the south, Vietnam's topography is a study in contrasts. In the north, the rugged mountains of the Hoang Lien Son range dominate the landscape, with the majestic Fansipan peak standing as the highest point in Indochina. This region is known for its terraced rice paddies, picturesque valleys, and vibrant ethnic minority cultures.

Moving southward, the landscape gradually flattens out into the fertile plains of the Red River Delta and the Mekong Delta. These vast river deltas are the breadbaskets of Vietnam, supporting a thriving agricultural industry and sustaining millions of livelihoods. The Mekong Delta, in particular, is a labyrinth of waterways, rice fields, and floating markets, offering a glimpse into traditional Vietnamese rural life.

Along Vietnam's extensive coastline, stunning beaches, and picturesque islands beckon travelers seeking sun, sand, and sea. From the pristine shores of Phu Quoc in the south to the emerald waters of Ha Long Bay in the north, Vietnam's coastal regions are renowned for their natural beauty and biodiversity. Ha Long Bay, a UNESCO World Heritage Site, is famous for its towering limestone karsts, hidden caves, and turquoise waters, making it a must-visit destination for travelers from around the world.

Vietnam's climate is as varied as its geography, with distinct weather patterns prevailing across different regions of the country. In the north, the climate is characterized by four seasons, with cold winters and hot, humid summers. Central Vietnam experiences a tropical monsoon climate, with heavy rainfall during the wet season from September to December. The south enjoys a tropical climate year-round, with high temperatures and humidity moderated by the southwest monsoon from May to October.

Despite the diversity of its landscapes and weather patterns, Vietnam is united by its natural beauty and rich biodiversity. From lush forests and mangrove swamps to vast wetlands and coral reefs, Vietnam's ecosystems are home to a wealth of plant and animal species, many of which are endemic to the region. Protecting and preserving this natural heritage is essential for the future of Vietnam and the well-being of its people.

Flora and Fauna: Exploring Vietnam's Biodiversity

Vietnam's biodiversity is a treasure trove of life, boasting a rich tapestry of flora and fauna that spans diverse ecosystems from lush rainforests to towering mountain ranges. With its strategic location in Southeast Asia and varied topography, Vietnam is home to an astonishing array of plant and animal species, many of which are found nowhere else on Earth.

In the dense tropical rainforests of Vietnam's central highlands and northern regions, towering trees and dense undergrowth provide habitat for a myriad of plant species. These forests are home to rare and endangered species such as the Vietnamese giant muntjac, the Annamite striped rabbit, and the saola, also known as the Asian unicorn due to its elusive nature. The towering trees of Vietnam's rainforests also support a rich diversity of bird species, including colorful parrots, hornbills, and pheasants.

Moving southward into the wetlands and mangrove forests of the Mekong Delta, Vietnam's biodiversity takes on a different character. Here, vast expanses of rice paddies, marshes, and waterways provide habitat for a wide variety of aquatic and semi-aquatic species. The Mekong River itself is one of the most biologically diverse river systems in the world, supporting hundreds of fish species, including the iconic Mekong giant catfish and the elusive Irrawaddy dolphin.

Vietnam's coastal regions are also teeming with life, with extensive coral reefs, seagrass beds, and mangrove forests providing habitat for a diverse array of marine species. These ecosystems are home to colorful coral reefs, sea turtles, dolphins, and a multitude of fish species, making Vietnam a popular destination for snorkeling, diving, and marine ecotourism.

In addition to its terrestrial and marine biodiversity, Vietnam is also home to a wealth of endemic plant species, many of which have medicinal or cultural significance. The country's forests are rich in biodiversity, with thousands of plant species, including orchids, ferns, and bamboo, as well as rare and endangered species such as the Vietnamese golden cypress and the Vietnamese pitcher plant.

Protecting and preserving Vietnam's biodiversity is essential for the country's future and the well-being of its people. Efforts to conserve key habitats, establish protected areas, and combat illegal wildlife trade are underway, but more needs to be done to ensure the long-term sustainability of Vietnam's natural heritage. By celebrating and safeguarding its biodiversity, Vietnam can continue to thrive as a nation of natural wonders and ecological diversity.

Vietnamese Cuisine: A Culinary Adventure

Vietnamese cuisine is a vibrant tapestry of flavors, textures, and aromas that reflects the country's rich cultural heritage and diverse culinary traditions. Known for its fresh ingredients, bold spices, and balance of flavors, Vietnamese food is celebrated around the world for its complexity and depth.

At the heart of Vietnamese cuisine is the concept of "ngon," which translates to deliciousness or tastiness. Vietnamese cooks strive to create dishes that are harmonious in flavor, with a careful balance of sweet, sour, salty, bitter, and umami tastes. This emphasis on balance is evident in iconic dishes such as pho, a fragrant noodle soup made with savory broth, rice noodles, and an array of herbs and toppings.

Rice is a staple of the Vietnamese diet and serves as the foundation for many dishes. Whether steamed, fried, or turned into noodles, rice plays a central role in Vietnamese cuisine, providing sustenance and texture to a wide variety of meals. In addition to rice, Vietnamese cuisine also features an abundance of fresh herbs, vegetables, and seafood, reflecting the country's agricultural abundance and coastal geography.

One of the hallmarks of Vietnamese cuisine is its use of fresh and seasonal ingredients. Vietnamese cooks take pride in sourcing the freshest produce and seafood available, often purchasing ingredients directly from local markets or growing them in their own gardens. This emphasis on freshness ensures that Vietnamese dishes burst with flavor and vitality, making each meal a memorable culinary experience.

Vietnamese cuisine is also characterized by its diverse range of cooking techniques, from stir-frying and steaming to grilling and braising. Each method imparts its own unique flavors and textures to the dish, resulting in a diverse array of culinary delights. Whether it's the smoky char of grilled meats, the delicate steam of dumplings, or the aromatic stir-fry of vegetables, Vietnamese cooking techniques are as varied as they are delicious.

In addition to its savory dishes, Vietnamese cuisine is also known for its delectable array of sweets and desserts. From delicate pastries and custards to refreshing fruit salads and shaved ice desserts, Vietnamese sweets offer a tantalizing end to any meal. Popular desserts include che, a sweet soup made with beans, fruits, and jelly, and banh chuoi, a banana cake often served with coconut milk.

Vietnamese cuisine is a reflection of the country's rich history, diverse culture, and bountiful natural resources. Whether you're savoring a bowl of pho on the streets of Hanoi or enjoying a banh mi sandwich in Ho Chi Minh City, every bite tells a story of tradition, innovation, and culinary excellence. Embark on a culinary adventure through Vietnam and discover the flavors of this remarkable cuisine for yourself.

Must-Try Dishes: From Pho to Banh Mi

When it comes to Vietnamese cuisine, there's no shortage of delicious dishes to tantalize your taste buds. From comforting soups to savory sandwiches, Vietnam offers a culinary journey like no other.

Let's start with pho, perhaps the most iconic Vietnamese dish. This flavorful noodle soup is made with a rich, aromatic broth infused with spices like star anise, cinnamon, and cloves. Thin slices of beef or chicken are added to the steaming broth, along with rice noodles, fresh herbs, and a squeeze of lime. Pho is enjoyed at any time of day, but it's particularly popular as a hearty breakfast or late-night snack.

Another must-try dish is banh mi, a Vietnamese sandwich that combines French and Vietnamese culinary influences. Crispy baguette is filled with a tantalizing array of ingredients, including thinly sliced meats, pickled vegetables, fresh herbs, and spicy condiments. The result is a symphony of flavors and textures that has made banh mi a beloved street food favorite both in Vietnam and around the world.

For seafood lovers, there's nothing quite like cha ca la vong, a specialty of Hanoi. This dish features tender pieces of fish marinated in turmeric and grilled to perfection, then served with fresh herbs, vermicelli noodles, and a tangy dipping sauce. The combination of flavors is simply irresistible, making cha ca la vong a must-try for anyone visiting the Vietnamese capital.

If you're in the mood for something spicy, look no further than bun bo Hue, a spicy beef noodle soup from the city of Hue. This fiery dish features thick rice noodles swimming in a spicy broth flavored with lemongrass, shrimp paste, and chili oil. Topped with slices of beef, pork, and pork blood sausage, bun bo Hue is a hearty and satisfying meal that will warm you from the inside out.

And let's not forget about banh xeo, a crispy Vietnamese pancake filled with savory delights. Made from a batter of rice flour, coconut milk, and turmeric, banh xeo is cooked until golden and crispy, then filled with a mixture of shrimp, pork, bean sprouts, and herbs. Served with a side of fresh lettuce leaves and nuoc cham dipping sauce, banh xeo is a delightful combination of flavors and textures that is sure to please.

These are just a few of the must-try dishes that await you in Vietnam. Whether you're exploring the bustling streets of Hanoi, the vibrant markets of Ho Chi Minh City, or the tranquil countryside of Hue, be sure to indulge in the diverse and delicious flavors of Vietnamese cuisine. You won't be disappointed!

Traditional Ingredients and Cooking Techniques

Traditional Vietnamese cuisine is a harmonious blend of fresh ingredients and time-honored cooking techniques that have been passed down through generations. At the heart of Vietnamese cooking are a few key ingredients that form the foundation of many dishes. Rice, both white and sticky, is a staple of the Vietnamese diet, serving as the base for everything from steamed rice to rice noodles. Fish sauce, known as nuoc mam, is another essential ingredient, adding depth and complexity to dishes with its salty, savory flavor.

Herbs and aromatics play a crucial role in Vietnamese cuisine, adding brightness and freshness to dishes. Common herbs include cilantro, mint, Thai basil, and lemongrass, while aromatics like garlic, ginger, and shallots impart depth and flavor to sauces and marinades. Vegetables such as bean sprouts, water spinach, and bok choy are also widely used, adding texture and nutrients to dishes.

When it comes to cooking techniques, Vietnamese cuisine is characterized by its simplicity and attention to detail. Stir-frying is a common method, with ingredients quickly cooked in a wok over high heat to preserve their freshness and flavor. Steaming is another popular technique, especially for delicate seafood and dumplings, while boiling is used for soups and broths. Grilling and barbecuing are also common, particularly for meats and seafood, imparting a smoky flavor and charred exterior.

One of the most distinctive features of Vietnamese cooking is the emphasis on freshness and balance. Dishes are often light and healthy, with an emphasis on vegetables, herbs, and lean proteins. Flavors are carefully balanced to achieve the perfect combination of sweet, sour, salty, bitter, and umami tastes, creating a harmonious and satisfying dining experience.

Many traditional Vietnamese dishes are also labor-intensive, requiring careful preparation and attention to detail. Ingredients are often chopped finely, marinated, and cooked slowly to allow flavors to develop fully. This dedication to craftsmanship is evident in dishes like pho, where the broth is simmered for hours to extract maximum flavor from the bones and aromatics.

Overall, traditional Vietnamese cuisine is a celebration of fresh ingredients, bold flavors, and time-honored techniques. Whether you're savoring a bowl of fragrant noodle soup or biting into a crispy banh mi sandwich, each dish tells a story of tradition, culture, and culinary excellence.

Street Food Culture: Where to Find the Best Eats

Vietnam's street food culture is a vibrant and essential part of daily life, offering a tantalizing array of flavors and aromas that beckon locals and travelers alike. From bustling markets to hidden alleyways, the streets of Vietnam are alive with the sizzle of grills, the fragrance of herbs, and the chatter of hungry diners.

One of the best places to experience Vietnam's street food culture is in the bustling city of Hanoi, where sidewalk vendors set up makeshift stalls selling everything from fragrant noodle soups to crispy spring rolls. The Old Quarter is a particularly vibrant hub of street food activity, with narrow streets lined with stalls offering an endless variety of culinary delights.

In Ho Chi Minh City, also known as Saigon, the Ben Thanh Market is a must-visit destination for food lovers. Here, vendors hawk everything from banh mi sandwiches to steaming bowls of pho, while the surrounding streets come alive at night with colorful food stalls serving up grilled meats, seafood, and Vietnamese desserts.

For a taste of authentic Vietnamese seafood, head to the coastal city of Da Nang, where the My Khe Beach is lined with seafood restaurants and street vendors offering freshly caught fish, crab, and shellfish. Be sure to try the local specialty, banh xeo, a crispy pancake filled with shrimp, pork, and bean sprouts.

In the ancient town of Hoi An, the night market is a food lover's paradise, with vendors selling a tantalizing array of street food snacks and local specialties. Be sure to sample cao lau, a unique noodle dish made with chewy rice noodles, tender slices of pork, and fragrant herbs, all topped with crispy croutons.

No visit to Vietnam would be complete without exploring the street food scene in the Mekong Delta, where floating markets and riverside stalls offer a glimpse into traditional Vietnamese life. Here, you can sample fresh tropical fruits, grilled fish, and other regional specialties while taking in the sights and sounds of this picturesque region.

Whether you're exploring the bustling streets of Hanoi, the vibrant markets of Ho Chi Minh City, or the tranquil countryside of the Mekong Delta, Vietnam's street food culture offers a delicious and immersive culinary experience that is not to be missed. So grab a stool, pull up to a roadside stall, and prepare to embark on a gastronomic adventure through the streets of Vietnam.

Iconic Sights: Exploring Vietnam's Top Tourist Attractions

Vietnam is a land of breathtaking natural beauty and rich cultural heritage, home to a wealth of iconic sights that draw millions of visitors from around the world each year. From ancient temples to stunning natural landscapes, there's no shortage of must-see attractions to explore in this diverse and captivating country.

One of Vietnam's most famous landmarks is Ha Long Bay, a UNESCO World Heritage Site renowned for its emerald waters, towering limestone karsts, and hidden caves. A cruise through Ha Long Bay offers visitors the chance to marvel at the otherworldly beauty of this natural wonder, with opportunities for kayaking, swimming, and exploring the many islands and grottoes that dot the bay.

In the heart of Vietnam, the ancient city of Hoi An enchants visitors with its well-preserved architecture, vibrant lantern-lit streets, and rich cultural heritage. The historic old town is a UNESCO World Heritage Site, with narrow alleys lined with centuries-old buildings, traditional wooden houses, and atmospheric temples. Hoi An is also famous for its colorful lantern festival, held monthly on the night of the full moon, where the streets come alive with music, dance, and festivities.

For history buffs, the Imperial City of Hue offers a fascinating glimpse into Vietnam's royal past. Situated along the Perfume River, Hue was once the capital of the Nguyen Dynasty and is home to a wealth of historic sites, including the imposing Citadel, royal tombs, and ancient pagodas. A visit to Hue is like stepping back in time, with its evocative ruins and grand architecture providing a window into Vietnam's imperial history.

In the bustling metropolis of Ho Chi Minh City, formerly known as Saigon, visitors can explore a mix of modern and historic attractions. The War Remnants Museum offers a sobering look at the Vietnam War, with exhibits documenting the conflict and its impact on the country and its people. Nearby, the Notre Dame Cathedral and the Central Post Office are reminders of Vietnam's colonial past, while the bustling Ben Thanh Market offers a taste of local life and culture.

In the north, the ancient capital of Hanoi beckons with its charming old quarter, historic landmarks, and vibrant street life. The Hoan Kiem Lake is a focal point of the city, with its tranquil waters and iconic red bridge, while the nearby Temple of Literature is a testament to Vietnam's scholarly heritage. Hanoi is also home to the mausoleum of Ho Chi Minh, the revered leader of Vietnam's struggle for independence, where visitors can pay their respects to the country's founding father.

These are just a few of the iconic sights that await you in Vietnam. Whether you're exploring the natural wonders of Ha Long Bay, immersing yourself in the history of Hue, or experiencing the vibrant culture of Hoi An and Ho Chi Minh City, Vietnam offers a wealth of unforgettable experiences for travelers of all interests and backgrounds.

Ha Long Bay: A Natural Wonder

Ha Long Bay stands as one of Vietnam's most awe-inspiring natural wonders, captivating visitors with its ethereal beauty and mystical charm. Located in the Gulf of Tonkin, off the coast of northeastern Vietnam, Ha Long Bay is renowned for its emerald waters, towering limestone karsts, and hidden caves. The bay covers an area of over 1,500 square kilometers, with thousands of limestone islands and islets rising dramatically from the sea.

These towering limestone formations, sculpted by millions of years of erosion, create a breathtaking seascape that is unlike anywhere else on earth. Some of the karsts soar hundreds of feet into the air, while others are adorned with lush vegetation and hidden lagoons. Each island seems to have its own unique personality, with names like Dragon, Fighting Cock, and Stone Dog Island reflecting their distinctive shapes and features.

One of the best ways to experience Ha Long Bay is by taking a cruise through its emerald waters. From the deck of a traditional junk boat, visitors can marvel at the otherworldly beauty of the karsts, with opportunities to explore hidden caves, swim in secluded lagoons, and kayak through labyrinthine waterways. As the sun sets over the bay, the limestone formations take on a golden hue, casting a magical spell over all who behold them.

Ha Long Bay is also home to a rich diversity of marine life, including colorful coral reefs, tropical fish, and rare sea creatures. The bay's clear waters provide excellent conditions for snorkeling and diving, with underwater caves, tunnels, and grottoes waiting to be explored. Lucky visitors may even spot dolphins, sea turtles, and the elusive dugong, a rare marine mammal that is native to the area.

In addition to its natural beauty, Ha Long Bay is also steeped in legend and folklore. According to Vietnamese mythology, the bay was formed by dragons sent by the gods to protect the country from invaders. These dragons spat out jewels and jade, which turned into the islands and islets that dot the bay, creating a natural fortress that kept Vietnam safe from harm.

Today, Ha Long Bay is recognized as a UNESCO World Heritage Site, revered for its outstanding natural beauty and geological significance. Despite its popularity as a tourist destination, the bay remains remarkably unspoiled, with efforts underway to preserve and protect its fragile ecosystem for future generations to enjoy. Whether you're cruising through its mystical waters, exploring its hidden caves, or simply marveling at its breathtaking vistas, Ha Long Bay is sure to leave a lasting impression on all who visit.

Ho Chi Minh City (Saigon): A Vibrant Metropolis

Ho Chi Minh City, formerly known as Saigon, is a bustling metropolis that pulsates with energy, culture, and history. As the largest city in Vietnam, Ho Chi Minh City is a vibrant melting pot of tradition and modernity, where gleaming skyscrapers stand alongside ancient temples and bustling markets. Named after the revered leader of Vietnam's struggle for independence, Ho Chi Minh City is a testament to the country's resilience and determination in the face of adversity.

One of the most iconic landmarks in Ho Chi Minh City is the Notre Dame Cathedral, a beautiful neo-Romanesque church that dates back to the late 19th century. Built by French colonists, the cathedral is a symbol of Vietnam's colonial past and stands as a reminder of the country's rich cultural heritage. Nearby, the Central Post Office is another architectural gem, designed by the renowned architect Gustave Eiffel and featuring a stunning interior adorned with ornate decorations and mosaic tiles. For a taste of local life and culture, there's no better place to visit than the bustling Ben Thanh Market. Located in the heart of the city, this sprawling market is a labyrinth of narrow alleys and bustling stalls selling everything from fresh produce and seafood to handicrafts and souvenirs. Bargaining is the name of the game here, so be prepared to haggle for the best prices on everything from silk scarves to hand-carved wooden figurines. Ho Chi Minh City is also home to a thriving culinary scene, with a dizzying array of street food stalls, traditional eateries, and international restaurants to choose from. From fragrant noodle soups to crispy spring rolls, the city offers a culinary adventure like no other, with flavors and aromas that will tantalize your taste buds and leave you craving more.

In addition to its historic landmarks and culinary delights, Ho Chi Minh City is also a hub of cultural activity, with museums, galleries, and theaters showcasing the best of Vietnamese art and culture. The War Remnants Museum offers a sobering look at the Vietnam War, with exhibits documenting the conflict and its impact on the country and its people. Meanwhile, the Saigon Opera House is a stunning example of French colonial architecture and hosts a variety of performances, from classical music concerts to traditional Vietnamese theater.

Whether you're exploring the historic landmarks of District 1, sampling street food in the bustling neighborhoods of District 5, or taking in the sights and sounds of the city from the back of a motorbike taxi, Ho Chi Minh City is a vibrant metropolis that offers something for everyone. Soak up the energy, immerse yourself in the culture, and prepare to be captivated by the magic of this dynamic city.

Hanoi: Capital City Rich in History

Hanoi, the capital city of Vietnam, is a captivating blend of ancient traditions, colonial charm, and modern vitality. With a history spanning over a thousand years, Hanoi is one of the oldest continuously inhabited cities in Southeast Asia, boasting a rich cultural heritage and a wealth of historic landmarks.

At the heart of Hanoi lies the Hoan Kiem Lake, a picturesque body of water that has been a focal point of the city for centuries. Legend has it that the lake is home to a mythical giant turtle, and the Ngoc Son Temple, located on a small island in the middle of the lake, is dedicated to honoring this legendary creature. Surrounding the lake are tree-lined promenades, bustling markets, and historic buildings, creating a tranquil oasis in the heart of the bustling city.

One of the most iconic landmarks in Hanoi is the Temple of Literature, a sprawling complex of temples, pavilions, and courtyards that served as Vietnam's first university. Founded in 1070, the Temple of Literature is dedicated to Confucius and honors scholars and academics who have made significant contributions to Vietnamese culture and society. The temple's serene gardens and ancient stone steles make it a popular destination for locals and tourists alike. Hanoi is also home to the Ho Chi Minh Mausoleum, a monumental structure that serves as the final resting place of the revered leader of Vietnam's struggle for independence. Ho Chi Minh, affectionately known as "Uncle Ho" by the Vietnamese people, is a national hero and a symbol of the country's resilience and determination in the face of adversity. Visitors can pay their respects to Ho Chi Minh by viewing his embalmed body, which lies in state in the mausoleum's solemn interior.

In addition to its historic landmarks, Hanoi is also renowned for its vibrant street life and bustling markets. The Old Quarter, with its narrow streets and ancient architecture, is a maze of alleyways and alleys that are home to a dizzying array of street food stalls, traditional eateries, and handicraft shops. Here, visitors can sample local delicacies like pho, banh mi, and bun cha, while soaking up the sights and sounds of this bustling neighborhood.

Throughout its long and storied history, Hanoi has been shaped by a diverse array of cultural influences, from Chinese and French colonial rule to Vietnamese nationalism and independence. Today, the city is a vibrant metropolis that celebrates its past while embracing the future, offering visitors a unique blend of old-world charm and modern vitality. Whether you're exploring its ancient temples, strolling along its tree-lined boulevards, or sampling its culinary delights, Hanoi is a city that never fails to captivate and inspire.

Hue: Imperial City and Cultural Heartland

Nestled along the banks of the Perfume River in central Vietnam, Hue stands as a testament to the country's imperial past and cultural heritage. As the former capital of the Nguyen Dynasty, Hue served as the political, cultural, and religious center of Vietnam for over 140 years, leaving behind a legacy of grand palaces, ornate temples, and ancient pagodas.

One of the most iconic landmarks in Hue is the Imperial City, a vast complex of palaces, temples, and administrative buildings that served as the seat of power for the Nguyen emperors. Surrounded by massive stone walls and a moat, the Imperial City is a masterpiece of Vietnamese architecture, with its intricate gates, pavilions, and gardens reflecting the grandeur and majesty of the imperial court.

Within the Imperial City lies the Forbidden Purple City, a private enclave reserved for the emperor and his family. Accessible only to the most trusted servants and advisors, the Forbidden Purple City was once home to the imperial residences, ceremonial halls, and royal gardens. Today, visitors can explore the ruins of this once-glorious complex, marveling at its ornate architecture and rich history.

Another highlight of Hue is the complex of royal tombs scattered throughout the surrounding countryside. Built as lavish mausoleums for the Nguyen emperors, these tombs are architectural marvels, blending traditional Vietnamese design with elements of Chinese and French influence. Each tomb is unique, with its own distinctive style and symbolism, reflecting the personality and achievements of the emperor for whom it was built.

In addition to its imperial heritage, Hue is also known for its vibrant cultural scene, with a wealth of museums, galleries, and theaters showcasing the best of Vietnamese art and culture. The Hue Royal Antiquities Museum offers a fascinating glimpse into the lives of the Nguyen emperors, with its collection of royal artifacts, costumes, and treasures. Meanwhile, the Hue Festival, held biennially, celebrates the city's cultural heritage with a dazzling array of music, dance, and traditional performances.

Hue's rich history and cultural significance have earned it recognition as a UNESCO World Heritage Site, ensuring that its treasures will be preserved and protected for future generations to enjoy. Whether you're exploring the grandeur of the Imperial City, wandering through the tranquil gardens of a royal tomb, or immersing yourself in the vibrant arts scene, Hue is a city that offers a captivating blend of history, culture, and natural beauty.

Hoi An: Ancient Town of Lanterns and Traditions

Nestled along the banks of the Thu Bon River in central Vietnam, Hoi An is a charming and picturesque town that enchants visitors with its ancient architecture, lantern-lit streets, and rich cultural heritage. With a history dating back over a thousand years, Hoi An has served as a vital trading port, a bustling commercial center, and a melting pot of cultures and traditions.

At the heart of Hoi An lies the historic Old Town, a UNESCO World Heritage Site that boasts a well-preserved collection of centuries-old buildings, narrow alleyways, and bustling markets. The town's architecture reflects its diverse cultural influences, with Chinese temples, Japanese merchant houses, and French colonial villas standing side by side along its quaint streets.

One of the most iconic features of Hoi An is its vibrant lanterns, which adorn the streets, buildings, and riverbanks, casting a warm and enchanting glow over the town. Traditionally made from silk and bamboo, these colorful lanterns are crafted by skilled artisans using age-old techniques passed down through generations. The lanterns are not only a symbol of Hoi An's cultural heritage but also play a practical role in illuminating the town's streets and alleyways at night.

Hoi An is also known for its rich culinary traditions, with a diverse array of local dishes and specialties to tempt the palate. From fragrant noodle soups to crispy spring rolls, Hoi An's street food stalls and traditional eateries offer a tantalizing taste of Vietnamese cuisine. The town is particularly famous for its cao lau, a unique noodle dish made with chewy rice noodles, tender slices of pork, and fragrant herbs, all topped with crispy croutons.

In addition to its culinary delights, Hoi An is also a paradise for shoppers and artisans, with its bustling markets and artisan workshops showcasing a wide variety of handmade crafts and traditional goods. Visitors can browse through the colorful stalls of the Central Market, haggle for souvenirs and handicrafts, or even try their hand at lantern-making or silk weaving under the guidance of local artisans.

Beyond its ancient town center, Hoi An is also blessed with stunning natural scenery, with pristine beaches, lush countryside, and tranquil rivers waiting to be explored. The nearby Cua Dai Beach offers miles of golden sand and crystal-clear waters, perfect for swimming, sunbathing, and water sports. Meanwhile, the surrounding countryside is dotted with picturesque rice paddies, coconut groves, and traditional fishing villages, providing a peaceful escape from the hustle and bustle of the town center.

With its ancient charm, vibrant culture, and natural beauty, Hoi An is a destination that captivates the imagination and leaves a lasting impression on all who visit. Whether you're wandering through its historic streets, sampling its delicious cuisine, or simply soaking up the atmosphere, Hoi An is a town that invites you to slow down, savor the moment, and embrace the magic of its timeless beauty.

Da Nang: Gateway to Central Vietnam

Situated along the central coast of Vietnam, Da Nang serves as a bustling gateway to the cultural and natural wonders of Central Vietnam. With its strategic location between the ancient cities of Hue and Hoi An, Da Nang has long been an important commercial and transportation hub, connecting the north and south of the country.

One of the most iconic landmarks in Da Nang is the Dragon Bridge, a stunning architectural marvel that spans the Han River. Shaped like a dragon, the bridge is illuminated at night with colorful LED lights, creating a dazzling spectacle that has become a symbol of the city. Every weekend, the Dragon Bridge comes to life with a spectacular fire-breathing display, delighting locals and visitors alike.

Another must-visit attraction in Da Nang is the Marble Mountains, a cluster of five limestone hills that rise dramatically from the flat coastal plain. Each of the mountains is named after one of the five elements – water, wood, fire, metal, and earth – and is home to a network of caves, pagodas, and shrines. Visitors can climb to the summit of Thuy Son, the largest and most famous of the mountains, to enjoy panoramic views of the surrounding countryside and coastline.

For beach lovers, Da Nang boasts some of the most beautiful stretches of coastline in Vietnam. My Khe Beach, also known as China Beach, is a long, sandy expanse that stretches for miles along the coast, offering pristine waters, gentle waves, and plenty of opportunities for swimming, sunbathing, and water sports. Nearby, Non Nuoc Beach is famous for its white sand and clear waters, making it a popular destination for both locals and tourists alike.

Da Nang is also home to a thriving culinary scene, with a wide variety of local specialties and international cuisines to tempt the taste buds. The city's bustling streets and vibrant markets are filled with food stalls and restaurants serving up everything from fresh seafood and grilled meats to noodle soups and banh mi sandwiches. Be sure to try some of the local favorites, such as mi quang, a hearty noodle dish made with turmeric-infused broth, and banh xeo, a crispy pancake filled with shrimp, pork, and bean sprouts.

With its stunning natural beauty, rich cultural heritage, and vibrant atmosphere, Da Nang offers a taste of everything that makes Vietnam such a captivating destination. Whether you're exploring its ancient pagodas, lounging on its pristine beaches, or sampling its delicious cuisine, Da Nang is sure to leave a lasting impression on all who visit.

Nha Trang: Beach Paradise and Water Activities

Nha Trang, nestled along the stunning coastline of southern Vietnam, is renowned as a beach paradise and a haven for water activities enthusiasts. With its crystal-clear waters, golden sands, and vibrant marine life, Nha Trang attracts visitors from around the world seeking sun, sea, and adventure.

At the heart of Nha Trang lies its main beach, a long stretch of soft, white sand that gently slopes into the warm waters of the South China Sea. The beach is lined with palm trees and dotted with colorful umbrellas, providing plenty of shade for sunbathers and a picturesque backdrop for beachgoers. Whether you're lounging on a beach chair, building sandcastles with the kids, or simply taking a leisurely stroll along the shoreline, Nha Trang's main beach offers the perfect setting for relaxation and recreation.

For those seeking more active pursuits, Nha Trang offers a wide range of water activities to suit every taste and skill level. Snorkeling and scuba diving are popular choices, with the vibrant coral reefs and abundant marine life of Nha Trang's offshore islands providing some of the best diving opportunities in Vietnam. Whether you're a seasoned diver or a first-time snorkeler, the clear waters of Nha Trang offer a mesmerizing underwater world just waiting to be explored.

In addition to diving and snorkeling, Nha Trang is also a paradise for water sports enthusiasts, with options ranging from jet skiing and parasailing to windsurfing and kitesurfing. The city's favorable weather conditions and steady sea breezes make it an ideal destination for these adrenaline-pumping activities, with plenty of rental shops and tour operators offering equipment and instruction for beginners and experienced thrill-seekers alike.

For a more leisurely experience on the water, visitors can take a boat tour of Nha Trang Bay, one of the most beautiful bays in the world. From the deck of a traditional wooden boat, you can cruise past picturesque islands, hidden coves, and secluded beaches, with opportunities for swimming, snorkeling, and sunbathing along the way. Sunset cruises are particularly popular, offering breathtaking views of the bay bathed in the golden glow of the setting sun.

Away from the water, Nha Trang offers plenty of attractions and activities to keep visitors entertained. The city's vibrant nightlife scene comes alive after dark, with beachfront bars, clubs, and restaurants offering live music, dancing, and entertainment late into the night. For a taste of local culture, be sure to visit the Po Nagar Cham Towers, a complex of ancient Hindu temples dating back over a thousand years, or the Long Son Pagoda, with its towering white Buddha statue overlooking the city.

Whether you're seeking relaxation, adventure, or a little bit of both, Nha Trang offers an unforgettable beach experience that is sure to leave you wanting more. So pack your swimsuit, grab your sunscreen, and get ready to soak up the sun and surf in one of Vietnam's most beautiful coastal destinations.

Mekong Delta: Exploring Vietnam's Rice Bowl

The Mekong Delta, often referred to as the "Rice Bowl" of Vietnam, is a vast and fertile region in the southern part of the country that is crisscrossed by a network of rivers, canals, and waterways. Covering an area of over 40,000 square kilometers, the Mekong Delta is one of the most important agricultural regions in Vietnam, producing a significant portion of the country's rice, fruit, and seafood.

The delta is formed by the Mekong River, one of the longest rivers in the world, which originates in the Tibetan Plateau and flows through China, Myanmar, Laos, Thailand, Cambodia, and Vietnam before emptying into the South China Sea. As the river meanders through the delta, it deposits nutrient-rich sediment, creating fertile soils that are ideal for agriculture.

One of the defining features of the Mekong Delta is its intricate system of waterways, which serve as both transportation routes and sources of irrigation for the region's rice fields and fruit orchards. Traveling by boat is a way of life in the delta, with colorful wooden boats plying the canals and rivers, ferrying goods and passengers between villages and towns. The Mekong Delta is also known for its vibrant floating markets, where farmers and traders gather to buy and sell goods directly from their boats. Cai Rang and Cai Be are two of the most famous floating markets in the delta, bustling with activity as vendors haggle over prices and shoppers peruse the colorful displays of fruits, vegetables, and other goods.

In addition to its agricultural significance, the Mekong Delta is also a haven for wildlife, with dense mangrove forests, wetlands, and marshes providing habitat for a diverse array of plant and animal species. The delta is home to over 1,000 species of fish, as well as rare birds, mammals, and reptiles, making it a popular destination for ecotourism and birdwatching.

Visitors to the Mekong Delta can explore its natural beauty and cultural heritage through a variety of activities, including boat tours, cycling excursions, and visits to local villages and farms. They can sample fresh fruit from orchards, watch traditional crafts being made, and learn about the unique way of life of the delta's inhabitants.

Whether you're cruising along its scenic waterways, sampling its delicious fruits, or immersing yourself in its rich cultural traditions, the Mekong Delta offers a fascinating glimpse into the heart and soul of Vietnam. It's a place where the rhythm of life is dictated by the ebb and flow of the mighty Mekong River, and where the bounty of the land sustains generations of hardworking farmers and fishermen.

Vietnamese Traditions and Customs: Etiquette and Social Norms

Vietnamese traditions and customs are deeply rooted in the country's rich history and cultural heritage, shaping the way people interact and conduct themselves in everyday life. Etiquette and social norms play a significant role in Vietnamese society, guiding behavior and fostering harmony and respect among individuals and communities.

One of the most important aspects of Vietnamese etiquette is the concept of respect for elders and authority figures. In Vietnamese culture, age and status are highly valued, and younger generations are expected to show deference and obedience to their elders. This is often demonstrated through gestures such as bowing or using formal language when addressing elders, as well as by following traditional customs and rituals that honor ancestors and ancestors.

Another key aspect of Vietnamese etiquette is the importance of saving face and avoiding confrontation or embarrassment in social situations. Vietnamese people place a high value on harmony and maintaining positive relationships with others, so it's important to avoid causing offense or embarrassment, even in difficult situations. This can sometimes lead to indirect communication and subtle expressions of disagreement or dissatisfaction, as open confrontation is generally considered impolite.

Hospitality is also a cornerstone of Vietnamese culture, with guests often treated with great warmth and generosity. Visitors to Vietnamese homes can expect to be greeted with a warm welcome and offered food, drink, and hospitality. It's customary to remove shoes before entering someone's home and to bring a small gift, such as fruit or flowers, as a token of appreciation for the hospitality.

Mealtime etiquette is another important aspect of Vietnamese customs, with shared meals serving as an opportunity for family and friends to come together and bond. Dining is typically a communal affair, with dishes served family-style and everyone helping themselves from a central serving platter. It's considered polite to wait for the host to begin eating before starting your meal, and to use chopsticks and a spoon rather than a fork and knife.

In addition to these general customs and traditions, there are also specific rituals and practices associated with special occasions and holidays in Vietnam. These may include ceremonies to honor ancestors, celebrate weddings or births, or mark important milestones in life. Participation in these rituals helps to reinforce cultural identity and strengthen social bonds within the community.

Overall, Vietnamese traditions and customs are a reflection of the country's deep cultural heritage and values, emphasizing respect for elders, harmony in social interactions, and hospitality towards others. By understanding and respecting these customs, visitors to Vietnam can gain a deeper appreciation for the country's culture and forge meaningful connections with its people.

Festivals and Celebrations: Colorful Cultural Experiences

Festivals and celebrations are integral parts of Vietnamese culture, offering colorful and vibrant experiences that showcase the country's rich traditions and heritage. Throughout the year, communities across Vietnam come together to celebrate a variety of religious, cultural, and seasonal events, each marked by its own unique customs, rituals, and festivities.

One of the most iconic festivals in Vietnam is Tet Nguyen Dan, or simply Tet, which marks the Lunar New Year and is the country's most important holiday. Celebrated over the course of several days in late January or early February, Tet is a time for families to come together, honor ancestors, and welcome the arrival of spring. Homes are decorated with flowers, fruit trees, and traditional ornaments, and special foods are prepared to symbolize luck, prosperity, and happiness in the coming year.

Another popular festival in Vietnam is the Mid-Autumn Festival, also known as Tet Trung Thu, which takes place on the 15th day of the eighth lunar month. Celebrated primarily by children and families, the Mid-Autumn Festival is a time for mooncakes, lanterns, and outdoor festivities. Children carry colorful lanterns through the streets, while families gather to enjoy mooncakes and other traditional treats, such as sticky rice cakes and fruit.

One of the most unique festivals in Vietnam is the Perfume Pagoda Festival, held annually at the Perfume Pagoda complex near Hanoi. Lasting from January to March, this pilgrimage festival attracts thousands of visitors who come to pray for health, prosperity, and good fortune in the coming year. The highlight of the festival is a boat ride along the Yen Stream to the Perfume Pagoda, where pilgrims climb a steep mountain path to visit the sacred shrines and temples nestled among the limestone cliffs.

In addition to these major festivals, Vietnam is also home to a wide variety of regional celebrations that highlight the country's diverse cultural heritage. From the colorful boat races of the Ha Long Bay Carnival to the vibrant lantern festivals of Hoi An, each festival offers a unique glimpse into the traditions and customs of its respective region.

Whether you're marveling at the fireworks and dragon dances of Tet, sampling mooncakes and admiring lanterns at the Mid-Autumn Festival, or joining pilgrims on a journey to the Perfume Pagoda, festivals and celebrations in Vietnam are a feast for the senses and an unforgettable experience for visitors and locals alike.

Vietnamese Art and Architecture: Beauty in Design

Vietnamese art and architecture are renowned for their beauty, intricacy, and cultural significance, reflecting the country's rich history and diverse influences. From ancient temples and pagodas to modern sculptures and paintings, Vietnamese artistry encompasses a wide range of styles, techniques, and mediums that have evolved over centuries.

One of the most striking features of Vietnamese architecture is its blend of indigenous, Chinese, and French influences, resulting in a unique and eclectic style that is distinctly Vietnamese. Traditional Vietnamese architecture is characterized by its use of wood, bamboo, and ceramics, with curved roofs, ornate carvings, and intricate motifs that symbolize prosperity, protection, and good fortune.

One of the most iconic examples of Vietnamese architecture is the Temple of Literature in Hanoi, a masterpiece of classical Vietnamese design that dates back to the 11th century. Built to honor Confucius and scholars, the temple complex features a series of courtyards, pavilions, and shrines set amidst lush gardens and tranquil ponds. Its traditional wooden structures and tiled roofs exemplify the elegance and harmony of Vietnamese architectural principles. Vietnamese art is also celebrated for its exquisite craftsmanship and attention to detail, with traditional techniques such as lacquerware, silk painting, and ceramics dating back centuries. Lacquerware, in particular, is a highly regarded art form in Vietnam, with artisans using layers of resin derived from the sap of the lacquer tree to create stunning decorative pieces that are both durable and beautiful.

Silk painting is another important aspect of Vietnamese art, with artists using delicate brushes and vibrant dyes to create intricate designs on silk fabric. These paintings often depict scenes from nature, mythology, and daily life, with an emphasis on fluid lines, harmonious colors, and a sense of balance and proportion.

In addition to traditional art forms, Vietnam also has a thriving contemporary art scene, with artists exploring a wide range of styles and mediums to express their creativity and vision. From abstract sculptures and avant-garde installations to politically charged paintings and multimedia performances, contemporary Vietnamese art reflects the country's dynamic culture and evolving identity in the modern world.

Whether you're exploring ancient temples and pagodas, admiring traditional crafts and artworks, or discovering the latest trends in contemporary art, Vietnamese art and architecture offer a feast for the senses and a window into the soul of this fascinating and vibrant country.

Traditional Music and Performing Arts

Traditional music and performing arts hold a special place in Vietnamese culture, serving as a vibrant expression of the country's history, beliefs, and values. With roots that stretch back thousands of years, Vietnamese music and performing arts encompass a wide range of genres, styles, and instruments that have evolved over time.

One of the most iconic forms of traditional Vietnamese music is đờn ca tài tử, a genre of folk music that originated in the southern region of Vietnam. Characterized by its melodic tunes, intricate rhythms, and soulful lyrics, đờn ca tài tử is often performed by small ensembles of musicians playing traditional instruments such as the đàn tranh (zither), đàn bầu (monochord), and đàn nguyệt (moon-shaped lute).

Another popular form of traditional music in Vietnam is nhạc cải lương, or Vietnamese opera, which combines elements of music, theater, and storytelling to depict historical events, legends, and moral tales. Nhạc cải lương features elaborate costumes, stylized movements, and emotive singing, with performers often using masks, fans, and other props to enhance the dramatic effect.

In addition to music, Vietnamese performing arts also include a variety of traditional dances, rituals, and ceremonies that are performed on special occasions and holidays. One of the most famous dances in Vietnam is the lion dance, which is often performed during festivals and celebrations to ward off evil spirits and bring good luck and prosperity to the community.

Vietnamese performing arts also include a rich tradition of puppetry, with water puppetry being one of the most unique and beloved forms of puppet theater in the country. Originating in the Red River Delta region of northern Vietnam, water puppetry involves intricate wooden puppets that are manipulated by puppeteers standing behind a screen submerged in water. The puppets appear to float and move gracefully across the water's surface, accompanied by live music and storytelling.

Overall, traditional music and performing arts play a vital role in Vietnamese culture, connecting people to their heritage and fostering a sense of community and belonging. Whether it's the soulful melodies of đờn ca tài tử, the dramatic performances of nhạc cải lương, or the enchanting puppetry of water puppet theater, Vietnamese music and performing arts continue to captivate audiences and inspire appreciation for the country's rich cultural heritage.

Religious Diversity: Buddhism, Confucianism, and more

Religious diversity in Vietnam is a fascinating aspect of the country's cultural landscape, with a rich tapestry of beliefs, practices, and traditions that have coexisted for centuries. Buddhism, Confucianism, Taoism, and Christianity are among the major religions practiced in Vietnam, each contributing to the country's unique spiritual heritage and shaping its social, ethical, and moral values.

Buddhism holds a prominent place in Vietnamese society, with a significant portion of the population identifying as Buddhists. Introduced to Vietnam over two millennia ago, Buddhism has become deeply intertwined with the country's culture and history, influencing everything from art and architecture to literature and philosophy. Vietnamese Buddhism encompasses a variety of traditions and sects, including Mahayana Buddhism, Theravada Buddhism, and Pure Land Buddhism, each with its own distinct practices and rituals.

Confucianism is another important philosophical and ethical system in Vietnam, emphasizing principles of morality, social order, and filial piety. Derived from the teachings of the Chinese philosopher Confucius, Confucianism has played a central role in shaping Vietnamese society, particularly in the realms of education, governance, and family life. Confucian values such as respect for authority, loyalty to family, and dedication to duty continue to influence Vietnamese culture to this day.

Taoism, with its emphasis on harmony with nature, spiritual cultivation, and the pursuit of balance and enlightenment, also has a presence in Vietnam, albeit to a lesser extent than Buddhism and Confucianism. Taoist temples and shrines can be found throughout the country, serving as places of worship and meditation for those who seek guidance and spiritual fulfillment.

In addition to these indigenous religions, Christianity has also made significant inroads in Vietnam, particularly in the southern regions of the country. Introduced by European missionaries in the 16th century, Christianity has since grown to become one of the largest religious communities in Vietnam, with both Roman Catholicism and Protestantism having sizable followings. Christian churches and cathedrals dot the Vietnamese landscape, offering spiritual refuge and community for believers.

Despite the diversity of religious beliefs in Vietnam, the country is known for its tradition of religious tolerance and pluralism, with followers of different faiths coexisting peacefully and often participating in each other's religious ceremonies and festivals. This spirit of inclusivity and mutual respect is a testament to the rich cultural heritage and shared values that unite the people of Vietnam, regardless of their religious beliefs.

Ethnic Minorities: Rich Tapestry of Cultures

Vietnam is home to a diverse array of ethnic minorities, each with its own unique cultural traditions, languages, and customs. While the majority of the population in Vietnam is of Kinh ethnicity, there are over 50 recognized ethnic minority groups scattered throughout the country, residing primarily in the mountainous regions of the north and central highlands.

Among the largest ethnic minority groups in Vietnam are the Hmong, Tay, Dao, and Thai people. The Hmong, known for their vibrant traditional clothing and intricate embroidery, are concentrated in the mountainous regions of northern Vietnam, where they practice subsistence farming and maintain a strong sense of community and identity. The Tay and Dao people, who also inhabit the northern highlands, are known for their skill in agriculture and handicrafts, producing beautiful textiles, pottery, and woodwork.

In the central highlands of Vietnam, the Bahnar, Ede, and Jarai people are among the most prominent ethnic minority groups. These communities have traditionally lived in close harmony with nature, relying on farming, hunting, and gathering for their livelihoods.

They have rich oral traditions, with storytelling, music, and dance playing important roles in their cultural heritage.

One of the most well-known ethnic minority groups in Vietnam is the Cham people, who primarily inhabit the central coastal regions of the country. The Cham are known for their distinctive architecture, including the iconic Cham towers, as well as their vibrant textiles, intricate wood carvings, and traditional dance performances. Despite centuries of assimilation and migration, the Cham have managed to preserve their unique cultural identity and religious practices, which are influenced by Hinduism and Islam.

In addition to these larger ethnic minority groups, Vietnam is also home to a multitude of smaller ethnic communities, each with its own language, customs, and way of life. From the Raglai people of the central highlands to the Khmer people of the Mekong Delta, these ethnic minorities contribute to the rich tapestry of cultures that make up the fabric of Vietnamese society.

Despite their cultural diversity, ethnic minority groups in Vietnam have faced challenges in preserving their traditions and way of life in the face of modernization and development. Efforts are underway to support and promote the cultural heritage of these communities, including initiatives to revitalize traditional crafts, preserve indigenous languages, and empower local artisans and practitioners.

Overall, the ethnic minorities of Vietnam represent a rich and vibrant mosaic of cultures, languages, and traditions that have endured for centuries. Their resilience and creativity contribute to the cultural richness and diversity of Vietnam, making the country a fascinating and dynamic destination for travelers and scholars alike.

Vietnamese Language: Basics and Common Phrases

The Vietnamese language, a member of the Austroasiatic language family, is the official language of Vietnam and is spoken by the majority of the country's population. It is known for its rich tonality, with six different tones that can completely change the meaning of a word. Vietnamese is written using the Latin alphabet, with additional diacritics to indicate tone.

Learning a few basic Vietnamese phrases can greatly enhance your travel experience in Vietnam and help you connect with locals. For example, "Xin chào" is the standard greeting, which means "hello" or "goodbye" depending on the context. "Cảm ơn" means "thank you," and "Xin lỗi" means "sorry" or "excuse me."

When addressing someone, it's polite to use their title followed by their first name. For example, "Anh" is used for older men, "Chị" for older women, "Em" for younger people, and "Cô" for unmarried women. "Ông" and "Bà" are used for older men and women, respectively, regardless of marital status.

If you're dining out, "Món này ngon" means "This dish is delicious," while "Tôi không ăn thịt" means "I don't eat meat" if you're vegetarian. Asking for the bill is simple: "Tính tiền" or "Xin tính tiền."

Navigating transportation is also important. "Xe ôm" refers to motorcycle taxis, while "Xe buýt" is a bus. If you're negotiating a fare, you can ask, "Bao nhiêu tiền?" which means "How much?"

Numbers are crucial for shopping and bargaining. "Một" is one, "Hai" is two, and so on. "Mười" is ten, "Mười một" is eleven, and "Mười hai" is twelve. "Mười tám" is eighteen, and "Mười chín" is nineteen.

Lastly, expressing gratitude is key in Vietnamese culture. Saying "Xin lỗi" to apologize or "Cảm ơn" to thank someone goes a long way in building rapport and showing respect. Learning these basic phrases can make your interactions with locals smoother and more enjoyable during your time in Vietnam.

Language Variation Across Regions

Language variation across regions is a fascinating aspect of Vietnamese linguistics, reflecting the country's diverse geography, history, and cultural influences. While standard Vietnamese, based on the dialect of Hanoi, serves as the official language of Vietnam, there are significant differences in pronunciation, vocabulary, and grammar among different regions of the country.

One of the most notable differences in language variation is in the pronunciation of certain sounds, particularly the tones. While standard Vietnamese has six tones, the exact pronunciation of these tones can vary depending on the region. For example, in the southern region of Vietnam, the tones tend to be flatter and more clipped compared to the more melodious tones of the north.

Vocabulary also varies across regions, with different words and expressions used to describe the same concepts or objects. This can be influenced by factors such as local dialects, historical contacts with neighboring countries, and regional customs and traditions. For example, the word for "rice" may be "cơm" in the north but "cơm" or "cơm trắng" in the south.

Grammar can also differ from region to region, with variations in sentence structure, word order, and verb conjugation. While the basic rules of Vietnamese grammar remain consistent across the country, there may be subtle differences in usage and syntax that reflect regional preferences and norms. For example, in some southern dialects, the use of certain particles or auxiliary verbs may differ from standard Vietnamese.

Regional accents are another aspect of language variation in Vietnam, with distinct pronunciation patterns and intonations that can help identify where a person is from. For example, speakers from the north may have a softer, more nasal accent, while speakers from the south may have a more relaxed and melodic accent. These accents can sometimes be strong enough to be considered separate dialects, particularly in remote or isolated areas.

Despite these variations, mutual intelligibility remains high across different regions of Vietnam, meaning that speakers from different parts of the country can generally understand each other with little difficulty. This is due in part to the standardization of Vietnamese through education, media, and government policies, which have helped to promote a unified national language while still preserving regional diversity.

Overall, language variation across regions adds depth and richness to the linguistic landscape of Vietnam, reflecting the country's complex history and cultural heritage. By embracing these differences and celebrating the diversity of Vietnamese language and dialects, we gain a deeper appreciation for the richness and complexity of Vietnamese culture.

Vietnamese Writing System: Characters and Alphabet

The Vietnamese writing system is a unique blend of characters and an alphabet, which reflects the country's complex linguistic history and cultural influences. Unlike some other Asian languages that rely solely on characters, such as Chinese, Vietnamese uses a modified version of the Latin alphabet, known as quốc ngữ, alongside a system of characters borrowed from Chinese, known as chữ Nôm.

Quốc ngữ, introduced by Portuguese missionaries in the 17th century and later standardized by French colonial authorities, consists of 29 letters, including both vowels and consonants, as well as additional diacritics to indicate tones. This alphabet allows for relatively straightforward phonetic representation of Vietnamese words and is widely used in modern writing, printing, and digital communication.

Chữ Nôm, on the other hand, is a system of characters derived from Chinese characters but adapted to represent Vietnamese words and sounds. Developed over centuries by Vietnamese scholars and intellectuals, chữ Nôm was used primarily for literary and scholarly purposes before falling out of widespread use in favor of quốc ngữ during the colonial period. Today, chữ Nôm is primarily of historical and cultural interest, although efforts are underway to preserve and revive this ancient writing system.

The Vietnamese writing system is known for its use of diacritics, or tone marks, to indicate the six distinct tones of the language. These tone marks are essential for distinguishing between words that would otherwise be homophones, given that Vietnamese is a tonal language where the pitch contour of a word can change its meaning entirely. For example, the word "ma" can mean "ghost," "mother," "horse," or "rice seedling" depending on the tone.

In addition to diacritics, Vietnamese writing also employs various orthographic conventions to denote certain sounds and linguistic features. For example, the letter "ê" is used to represent the sound [e], while the combination "ưo" represents the diphthong [ɨə]. Similarly, digraphs such as "ch," "gh," and "nh" represent distinct consonantal sounds that do not exist in English.

Overall, the Vietnamese writing system is a testament to the country's linguistic diversity and cultural heritage, with its unique blend of characters and alphabet reflecting centuries of interaction and exchange with neighboring countries and colonial powers. By mastering this writing system, learners gain insight into the richness and complexity of the Vietnamese language and its vibrant literary tradition.

Learning Vietnamese: Tips for Language Acquisition

Learning Vietnamese can be a rewarding and enriching experience, allowing you to connect more deeply with the culture, people, and history of Vietnam. While mastering any language requires time, dedication, and practice, there are several tips and strategies that can help you accelerate your language acquisition and make the process more enjoyable.

First and foremost, immerse yourself in the language as much as possible. This can involve listening to Vietnamese music, watching Vietnamese movies or TV shows, and engaging with native speakers through language exchange programs or conversation groups. Exposure to authentic spoken Vietnamese will help you develop your listening comprehension skills and become more comfortable with the rhythms and nuances of the language.

Practice speaking regularly, even if you're just starting out and your vocabulary is limited. Don't be afraid to make mistakes – speaking is an essential part of language learning, and the more you practice, the more confident you'll become. Find opportunities to engage in conversation with native speakers, whether it's ordering food at a restaurant, asking for directions, or striking up a conversation with a local.

Use flashcards or language learning apps to expand your vocabulary and reinforce your understanding of grammar and sentence structure. Repetition is key to memorization, so review your flashcards regularly and incorporate new words and phrases into your daily conversations and writing practice.

Focus on mastering the tones of Vietnamese, as they play a crucial role in communication and can significantly affect the meaning of words. Practice pronouncing the six tones – ngang (level), huyền (falling), sắc (rising), hỏi (dipping-rising), ngã (falling-rising), and nặng (heavy) – until you can produce them accurately and consistently.

Don't neglect reading and writing in Vietnamese, even if you primarily want to focus on speaking and listening skills. Reading texts in Vietnamese will help you expand your vocabulary, improve your comprehension, and become more familiar with the structure and conventions of written Vietnamese. Start with simple texts and gradually work your way up to more complex material as your proficiency improves.

Finally, be patient and persistent. Language learning is a gradual process, and it's normal to encounter challenges and setbacks along the way. Celebrate your progress, no matter how small, and stay motivated by setting realistic goals and tracking your improvement over time. With dedication, perseverance, and a positive attitude, you'll be well on your way to mastering Vietnamese and unlocking a world of new opportunities and experiences.

Daily Life in Vietnam: Urban vs. Rural

Daily life in Vietnam varies significantly between urban and rural areas, each offering its own unique experiences, challenges, and opportunities. In urban centers like Ho Chi Minh City and Hanoi, life is characterized by hustle and bustle, with crowded streets, skyscrapers, and a vibrant atmosphere. These cities are hubs of commerce, culture, and entertainment, attracting people from all walks of life seeking employment, education, and a better standard of living.

In urban areas, modern amenities and conveniences are readily available, including shopping malls, restaurants, cafes, and public transportation systems. Residents often lead fast-paced lives, juggling work, school, and social activities amidst the constant buzz of city life. Traffic congestion and pollution are common challenges in urban areas, particularly during rush hours, but many residents adapt by using motorcycles or public transit to navigate the city.

Rural life in Vietnam, on the other hand, is characterized by a slower pace and closer connection to nature. Villages and farming communities dot the countryside, where rice fields, fruit orchards, and water buffalo are a common sight. Daily routines in rural areas revolve around agricultural activities, with families working together to plant, tend, and harvest crops.

In rural areas, access to modern amenities may be more limited, with fewer shops, restaurants, and entertainment options available compared to urban centers. However, residents often enjoy a strong sense of community and camaraderie, with neighbors helping each other in times of need and celebrating traditional festivals and ceremonies together.

Education and healthcare services may also differ between urban and rural areas, with urban centers typically offering more resources and facilities. However, efforts are underway to improve access to education, healthcare, and infrastructure in rural areas, particularly through government initiatives and international aid programs.

Despite these differences, urban and rural life in Vietnam share common values and traditions rooted in the country's rich cultural heritage. Family is central to Vietnamese society, regardless of whether one lives in the city or the countryside, and traditional customs and rituals are observed and passed down from generation to generation.

Overall, whether you're exploring the vibrant streets of a bustling city or wandering through the tranquil countryside, daily life in Vietnam offers a diverse array of experiences and perspectives that reflect the country's dynamic and evolving identity. By embracing both the urban and rural aspects of Vietnamese life, travelers and residents alike can gain a deeper appreciation for the beauty and complexity of this fascinating country.

Transportation: Navigating Vietnam's Roads and Waterways

Transportation in Vietnam is a diverse and dynamic system that encompasses a variety of modes, including roads, railways, waterways, and air travel. Navigating Vietnam's roads can be an adventure in itself, with bustling cities, winding mountain passes, and scenic coastal highways providing a range of experiences for travelers and commuters alike.

Motorcycles are a ubiquitous sight on Vietnam's roads, particularly in urban areas where they are the primary mode of transportation for many residents. Motorbikes offer flexibility and maneuverability in navigating congested streets, and they are often used for short trips around town or for commuting to work or school. However, traffic can be chaotic at times, with a constant flow of motorcycles, bicycles, pedestrians, and vehicles vying for space on the road.

In addition to motorcycles, cars, buses, and trucks are also common on Vietnam's roads, especially in larger cities and along major highways. Public transportation options vary depending on the region, with cities like Hanoi and Ho Chi Minh City boasting extensive bus networks and modern commuter rail systems.

Long-distance buses and trains connect major cities and tourist destinations, offering affordable and convenient travel options for both locals and visitors.

Water transportation is also important in Vietnam, given its extensive network of rivers, canals, and coastal waterways. In cities like Hanoi and Ho Chi Minh City, ferries and water taxis provide an alternative mode of transport for crossing rivers and navigating congested areas. In rural areas, boats and sampans are used for fishing, transportation, and commuting between islands and riverine communities.

Vietnam's railways offer another mode of transportation for long-distance travel, with the country's North-South Railway connecting Hanoi in the north to Ho Chi Minh City in the south. The railway system provides a scenic and comfortable way to explore the country, passing through picturesque landscapes, historic towns, and cultural sites along the way.

Finally, air travel is an increasingly popular option for domestic and international travel in Vietnam, with several airports serving major cities and tourist destinations across the country. Domestic airlines offer frequent flights between Hanoi, Ho Chi Minh City, Da Nang, and other cities, making it easy to explore different regions of Vietnam in a short amount of time.

Overall, navigating Vietnam's roads and waterways offers a rich and varied experience, allowing travelers to immerse themselves in the country's diverse landscapes, cultures, and traditions. Whether you're cruising along the coast on a motorcycle, riding a train through the countryside, or taking a boat tour of the Mekong Delta, transportation in Vietnam is an essential part of the journey and an adventure in itself.

Education and Healthcare: Access and Challenges

Education and healthcare are two vital aspects of society in Vietnam, each facing its own set of access and challenges. In terms of education, Vietnam places a strong emphasis on learning and academic achievement, with a high literacy rate and a culture that values education as a pathway to success. The country has made significant strides in expanding access to education in recent decades, with primary and secondary education being compulsory and free for all children. However, challenges remain, particularly in rural and remote areas where schools may be under-resourced and teachers may lack training and support. Additionally, there is pressure on students to perform well on standardized tests, leading to a competitive and sometimes stressful learning environment.

In terms of healthcare, Vietnam has made progress in improving access to medical services and reducing poverty-related health disparities. The government has implemented various initiatives to expand healthcare coverage, including the introduction of universal health insurance and the construction of new hospitals and healthcare facilities. Despite these efforts, access to quality healthcare remains uneven, with disparities between urban and rural areas, as well as between wealthy and marginalized populations. Rural areas often face shortages of healthcare workers and medical equipment, while urban areas may struggle with overcrowded hospitals and long wait times for treatment.

Additionally, there are challenges related to the quality and affordability of healthcare services in Vietnam. While the country has made strides in providing basic healthcare services, there are concerns about the quality of care provided in some facilities, as well as the high out-of-pocket costs for patients. Many Vietnamese rely on private healthcare providers for specialized care, leading to disparities in access based on income and socioeconomic status. Furthermore, there are ongoing efforts to improve the quality of medical education and training for healthcare professionals, as well as to strengthen healthcare infrastructure and promote preventive healthcare measures.

Overall, education and healthcare are essential components of Vietnam's social development, with progress being made in expanding access and addressing disparities. However, challenges remain in ensuring equitable access to quality education and healthcare for all Vietnamese citizens, particularly those in rural and marginalized communities. By addressing these challenges and investing in human capital and healthcare infrastructure, Vietnam can continue to improve the well-being and prosperity of its people in the years to come.

Economy and Industry: Growth Sectors and Challenges

Vietnam's economy has experienced rapid growth and transformation in recent decades, emerging as one of the fastest-growing economies in Southeast Asia. The country has transitioned from a centrally planned economy to a socialist-oriented market economy, implementing economic reforms and liberalization policies that have spurred investment, trade, and industrial development.

One of the key drivers of Vietnam's economic growth is its manufacturing sector, which has become a major contributor to GDP and employment. The country has attracted significant foreign investment in manufacturing industries such as electronics, textiles, footwear, and automotive assembly, benefiting from its relatively low labor costs, strategic location, and favorable business environment. Vietnam is now a leading exporter of manufactured goods, with multinational corporations establishing production facilities and supply chains in the country.

In addition to manufacturing, Vietnam's agricultural sector remains an important part of the economy, employing a significant portion of the population and contributing to food security and rural livelihoods. The country is one of the world's largest producers of rice, coffee, and seafood, exporting agricultural products to markets around the globe. However, the agricultural sector faces challenges such as land degradation, water scarcity, and climate change, which threaten productivity and sustainability in the long term.

The services sector is also a growing part of Vietnam's economy, driven by rising domestic consumption, urbanization, and tourism. The country has seen significant investment in infrastructure, retail, finance, and hospitality, with cities like Hanoi and Ho Chi Minh City becoming vibrant hubs of commerce, culture, and entertainment. Tourism is a particularly promising sector, with Vietnam's natural beauty, cultural heritage, and affordable travel attracting millions of visitors each year.

Despite its economic successes, Vietnam faces several challenges that threaten its continued growth and development. These include infrastructure deficiencies, bureaucratic inefficiencies, corruption, income inequality, and environmental degradation. The government has implemented various reforms and initiatives to address these challenges, including infrastructure investment programs, anti-corruption measures, and environmental protection policies. However, progress has been uneven, and there is still work to be done to ensure inclusive and sustainable economic development for all Vietnamese citizens.

Overall, Vietnam's economy is dynamic and resilient, with strong growth potential driven by its youthful population, entrepreneurial spirit, and strategic position in the global economy. By addressing challenges and capitalizing on opportunities in key sectors, Vietnam can continue to thrive and emerge as a leading economic powerhouse in the region and beyond.

Social Issues: Poverty, Corruption, and Environmental Concerns

Vietnam, like many developing countries, grapples with a range of social issues that impact the well-being and livelihoods of its people. Poverty is a persistent challenge, particularly in rural and remote areas, where access to education, healthcare, and economic opportunities may be limited. While Vietnam has made significant progress in reducing poverty rates in recent decades, disparities remain between urban and rural areas, as well as among different socioeconomic groups. Efforts to address poverty include government poverty reduction programs, investment in infrastructure and social services, and initiatives to promote sustainable economic growth and employment opportunities.

Corruption is another significant social issue in Vietnam, affecting various sectors of society, including government, business, and law enforcement. Transparency International ranks Vietnam relatively low on its Corruption Perceptions Index, highlighting concerns about bribery, nepotism, and abuse of power. Corruption undermines trust in institutions, stifles economic development, and erodes public confidence in the rule of law. The Vietnamese government has implemented anti-corruption measures, including legal reforms, public awareness campaigns, and anti-corruption task forces, but challenges persist in combating systemic corruption and ensuring accountability at all levels of government and society.

Environmental concerns are also a pressing issue in Vietnam, driven by rapid urbanization, industrialization, and population growth. Pollution, deforestation, water scarcity, and climate change pose significant threats to public health, ecosystems, and livelihoods. Vietnam is vulnerable to natural disasters such as typhoons, floods, and droughts, which are exacerbated by environmental degradation and climate change. The government has launched initiatives to address environmental challenges, including laws and regulations to protect natural resources, promote renewable energy, and mitigate the impacts of climate change. However, implementation and enforcement remain key challenges, as does balancing economic development with environmental sustainability.

Overall, addressing social issues such as poverty, corruption, and environmental concerns requires a multi-faceted approach involving government action, civil society engagement, and international cooperation. By prioritizing social welfare, good governance, and environmental stewardship, Vietnam can work towards building a more equitable, prosperous, and sustainable society for all its citizens.

Tourism Trends: Sustainable Travel in Vietnam

Tourism in Vietnam has experienced significant growth in recent years, with the country emerging as a popular destination for travelers seeking rich cultural experiences, stunning landscapes, and delicious cuisine. As tourism numbers continue to rise, there is increasing attention on promoting sustainable travel practices that minimize negative impacts on the environment, communities, and cultural heritage sites.

One trend in sustainable tourism in Vietnam is the growing interest in ecotourism and nature-based experiences. Travelers are increasingly seeking out opportunities to explore Vietnam's diverse ecosystems, including its lush rainforests, pristine beaches, and biodiversity-rich national parks. Eco-friendly accommodations, such as eco-lodges and homestays, are gaining popularity among travelers looking to minimize their environmental footprint while immersing themselves in nature.

Cultural tourism is also a key focus of sustainable travel in Vietnam, with travelers eager to learn about the country's rich history, traditions, and cultural heritage. Community-based tourism initiatives offer visitors the chance to engage with local communities, participate in traditional activities, and support local artisans and craftsmen. By promoting cultural exchange and preserving cultural traditions, these initiatives contribute to sustainable development and the preservation of Vietnam's cultural heritage.

In addition to promoting responsible tourism practices, there is also a growing emphasis on environmental conservation and protection in the tourism industry. Sustainable tourism operators are implementing measures to reduce waste, conserve energy and water, and minimize pollution in their operations. Initiatives such as beach clean-ups, wildlife conservation projects, and carbon offset programs are also becoming more common, allowing travelers to actively contribute to environmental conservation efforts during their visit.

Furthermore, there is a focus on supporting sustainable livelihoods and economic development through tourism. Community-based tourism initiatives empower local communities by providing economic opportunities, preserving traditional skills and knowledge, and promoting cultural pride and identity. By investing in local businesses, supporting fair wages, and respecting indigenous rights, sustainable tourism contributes to poverty alleviation and inclusive growth in Vietnam.

Overall, sustainable travel is increasingly shaping the tourism landscape in Vietnam, with travelers, businesses, and government agencies working together to promote responsible tourism practices and ensure the long-term sustainability of the industry. By embracing sustainable tourism principles and prioritizing environmental conservation, cultural preservation, and community empowerment, Vietnam can continue to attract travelers from around the world while safeguarding its natural and cultural treasures for future generations to enjoy.

Adventure Tourism: Trekking, Cycling, and Water Sports

Adventure tourism in Vietnam offers a thrilling and diverse range of outdoor activities for travelers seeking adrenaline-pumping experiences and immersive encounters with nature. Trekking is one of the most popular adventure activities, with numerous trekking routes traversing Vietnam's rugged mountains, lush forests, and picturesque countryside. The northern regions of Sapa and Ha Giang are particularly renowned for their stunning trekking trails, which wind through terraced rice fields, ethnic minority villages, and scenic valleys. Experienced trekkers can tackle challenging routes, including the ascent of Fansipan, the highest peak in Indochina, while beginners can opt for shorter, more leisurely hikes suitable for all fitness levels.

Cycling is another exciting adventure activity in Vietnam, offering travelers the opportunity to explore the country's diverse landscapes, vibrant cities, and charming countryside on two wheels. Vietnam boasts a growing network of cycling routes, ranging from urban bike paths and coastal roads to mountainous trails and rural backroads. The Mekong Delta, with its flat terrain and network of waterways, is a popular destination for cycling tours, allowing cyclists to pedal through lush rice paddies, fruit orchards, and traditional villages while soaking up the sights and sounds of rural life.

Water sports enthusiasts will find plenty of opportunities for adventure in Vietnam's coastal waters, rivers, and lakes. Kayaking, canoeing, and stand-up paddleboarding are popular activities in destinations such as Ha Long Bay, Nha Trang, and Phong Nha-Ke Bang National Park, where travelers can paddle through stunning limestone karsts, hidden caves, and emerald-green lagoons. For thrill-seekers, white-water rafting and canyoning adventures await in the mountainous regions of central and northern Vietnam, where fast-flowing rivers and cascading waterfalls provide the perfect playground for adrenaline junkies.

In addition to trekking, cycling, and water sports, adventure seekers can also indulge in a variety of other adrenaline-fueled activities in Vietnam. Rock climbing enthusiasts can test their skills on limestone cliffs in Ha Long Bay and Cat Ba Island, while zip-lining and high ropes courses offer aerial adventures amidst the treetops of lush jungle canopy. For those seeking a truly unique experience, paragliding and hot air ballooning provide exhilarating opportunities to soar above Vietnam's stunning landscapes and take in breathtaking views from above.

Overall, adventure tourism in Vietnam offers something for everyone, whether you're a seasoned outdoor enthusiast or a first-time thrill-seeker. With its diverse terrain, rich cultural heritage, and warm hospitality, Vietnam is a paradise for adventure travelers looking to embark on unforgettable experiences and create lasting memories in one of Southeast Asia's most captivating destinations.

Vietnam's Role in Southeast Asia: Politics and Diplomacy

Vietnam's role in Southeast Asia is multifaceted and dynamic, shaped by its history, geography, and political aspirations. As one of the largest countries in the region both in terms of land area and population, Vietnam wields significant influence in Southeast Asian politics and diplomacy.

Politically, Vietnam is a socialist republic governed by the Communist Party of Vietnam (CPV), which has maintained a firm grip on power since the country's reunification in 1975. The CPV's leadership plays a central role in shaping Vietnam's domestic and foreign policies, with a focus on maintaining political stability, economic development, and national sovereignty.

In terms of diplomacy, Vietnam has pursued a foreign policy of "doi moi" or renovation, aimed at diversifying its diplomatic relationships and strengthening its ties with countries around the world. Vietnam is an active member of various regional and international organizations, including the Association of Southeast Asian Nations (ASEAN), the United Nations (UN), and the World Trade Organization (WTO). Within ASEAN, Vietnam plays a prominent role in shaping the organization's agenda and policies, advocating for regional integration, economic cooperation, and peaceful resolution of disputes.

Vietnam has also been actively involved in promoting dialogue and cooperation on issues such as maritime security, counterterrorism, and sustainable development within the ASEAN framework. Vietnam's relations with its neighbors are characterized by a combination of cooperation and competition, shaped by historical legacies, territorial disputes, and geopolitical considerations. While Vietnam maintains friendly relations with most Southeast Asian countries, tensions have occasionally arisen over territorial disputes in the South China Sea, particularly with China, which claims sovereignty over parts of the disputed waters.

In addition to its regional diplomacy, Vietnam has also sought to strengthen its ties with major powers such as the United States, Russia, Japan, and India, balancing between different geopolitical interests to safeguard its national security and economic interests. Vietnam's strategic location along key maritime routes and its growing economic clout have made it an increasingly important player in regional and global affairs.

Overall, Vietnam's role in Southeast Asia is characterized by its strategic significance, diplomatic pragmatism, and commitment to regional cooperation and integration. As the country continues to navigate complex geopolitical dynamics and pursue its development goals, its influence in shaping the future of Southeast Asia is likely to grow in the years to come.

International Relations: Vietnam's Global Partnerships

Vietnam's international relations are marked by a diverse network of global partnerships and diplomatic engagements that reflect its strategic interests, economic priorities, and historical ties. Over the years, Vietnam has cultivated relationships with countries across the globe, spanning Asia, Europe, the Americas, and beyond.

In Asia, Vietnam maintains close ties with neighboring countries such as China, Japan, South Korea, and India, as well as with members of regional organizations like ASEAN and the Asia-Pacific Economic Cooperation (APEC) forum. These relationships are crucial for Vietnam's economic development, security, and regional stability. Vietnam's strategic partnership with China, while marked by historical tensions and territorial disputes, also encompasses extensive economic cooperation, trade, and investment.

Vietnam's relations with major powers such as the United States, Russia, and the European Union (EU) are also significant. The United States and Vietnam have normalized diplomatic relations since the end of the Vietnam War in 1975 and have deepened ties through trade, security cooperation, and people-to-people exchanges. Russia has been a longstanding partner of Vietnam, with historical ties dating back to the Soviet era, and continues to play a role in Vietnam's defense, energy, and economic sectors. The European Union is another important partner for Vietnam, with extensive trade and investment ties, development cooperation, and dialogues on human rights and governance issues.

Beyond bilateral relationships, Vietnam is actively engaged in multilateral diplomacy through organizations such as the United Nations (UN), where it serves as a non-permanent member of the UN Security Council for the 2020-2021 term, and the World Trade Organization (WTO), where it has been a member since 2007. Vietnam also participates in various regional and sub-regional forums, including the Mekong-Lancang Cooperation Mechanism, the East Asia Summit (EAS), and the Comprehensive and Progressive Agreement for Trans-Pacific Partnership (CPTPP), to promote regional cooperation, economic integration, and dialogue on pressing regional and global issues.

Furthermore, Vietnam has expanded its diplomatic outreach to emerging partners in Africa, Latin America, and the Middle East, seeking to diversify its international partnerships and enhance cooperation in areas such as trade, investment, and development assistance. Vietnam's global partnerships reflect its status as a dynamic and increasingly influential player in the international arena, with a growing role in shaping regional and global affairs.

Vietnamese Diaspora: Communities

The Vietnamese diaspora, comprised of individuals and communities living outside of Vietnam, is a vibrant and diverse population with a rich cultural heritage and a deep connection to their homeland. The Vietnamese diaspora is one of the largest in the world, with significant communities established in countries across the globe, including the United States, France, Australia, Canada, and Cambodia, among others.

The origins of the Vietnamese diaspora can be traced back to different waves of migration throughout history, driven by factors such as war, political upheaval, economic opportunities, and family reunification. The largest and most well-known wave of migration occurred following the end of the Vietnam War in 1975, when hundreds of thousands of Vietnamese fled the country as refugees, seeking asylum in countries around the world. These refugees, known as "boat people," faced perilous journeys by sea and resettled in countries such as the United States, Canada, Australia, France, and Germany, where they established thriving communities and contributed to the cultural and economic fabric of their host countries.

In addition to the refugee diaspora, there are also significant Vietnamese communities that trace their roots to earlier waves of migration, such as laborers and students who traveled abroad for work or education opportunities in the colonial era and during periods of political instability in Vietnam's history. These communities have established strong ties with their host countries and have contributed to the cultural diversity and social cohesion of their local communities.

The Vietnamese diaspora is characterized by its diversity, with individuals and communities representing a wide range of ethnic, linguistic, and cultural backgrounds. While many members of the Vietnamese diaspora maintain strong ties to their homeland and preserve Vietnamese language, traditions, and customs, others have assimilated into their host societies and identify with multiple cultural identities.

The Vietnamese diaspora plays a significant role in fostering cultural exchange, promoting economic development, and strengthening diplomatic ties between Vietnam and its host countries. Members of the diaspora contribute to Vietnam's economy through remittances, investments, and entrepreneurship, while also serving as cultural ambassadors and advocates for Vietnamese interests on the global stage.

Furthermore, the Vietnamese diaspora is actively engaged in philanthropy, community development, and advocacy efforts to support their homeland and address pressing issues such as human rights, social justice, and environmental conservation in Vietnam. Organizations and networks of Vietnamese diaspora communities around the world work together to promote cultural heritage preservation, language education, and solidarity among members of the diaspora and their descendants.

Overall, the Vietnamese diaspora is a dynamic and resilient community that continues to evolve and thrive, maintaining strong connections to Vietnam while contributing to the social, economic, and cultural vibrancy of their host countries and the global community.

Future Outlook: Opportunities and Challenges

The future outlook for Vietnam is filled with both opportunities and challenges, reflecting the country's dynamic and rapidly evolving socio-economic landscape. On one hand, Vietnam has experienced impressive economic growth over the past few decades, emerging as one of the fastest-growing economies in Southeast Asia and attracting significant foreign investment in key sectors such as manufacturing, technology, and services. The country's young and increasingly educated workforce, coupled with its strategic location and favorable business environment, position Vietnam as an attractive destination for both domestic and international investors looking to capitalize on its potential.

Moreover, Vietnam's integration into the global economy through trade agreements such as the Comprehensive and Progressive Agreement for Trans-Pacific Partnership (CPTPP) and the European Union-Vietnam Free Trade Agreement (EVFTA) presents new opportunities for export-driven growth, market expansion, and economic diversification. These agreements open up access to new markets, facilitate cross-border trade and investment, and promote greater economic cooperation and integration with regional and international partners.

At the same time, Vietnam faces a number of pressing challenges that must be addressed in order to sustain its economic growth and development trajectory. One of the key challenges is the need to enhance the country's infrastructure, particularly in areas such as transportation, energy, and telecommunications, to support continued economic expansion and improve living standards for its growing population. Investing in infrastructure development will require significant resources and strategic planning to address bottlenecks, inefficiencies, and gaps in the existing infrastructure network.

Additionally, Vietnam must address social and environmental issues such as income inequality, poverty, pollution, and climate change, which pose risks to sustainable development and social stability. Tackling these challenges will require coordinated efforts from government, businesses, civil society, and the international community to implement policies and initiatives that promote inclusive growth, environmental sustainability, and social equity.

Furthermore, Vietnam must navigate geopolitical dynamics and regional tensions, particularly in the South China Sea, where territorial disputes and competing claims have the potential to disrupt regional stability and economic cooperation. Managing relations with neighboring countries, major powers, and international organizations will be crucial for safeguarding Vietnam's sovereignty, security, and national interests while promoting peaceful resolution of disputes and upholding the rule of law.

In conclusion, the future outlook for Vietnam is characterized by a mix of opportunities and challenges that will shape the country's development trajectory in the years to come. By capitalizing on its strengths, addressing key challenges, and seizing opportunities for innovation, reform, and cooperation, Vietnam can position itself for continued growth, prosperity, and success in the global arena.

Epilogue

In this epilogue, we reflect on the journey through the diverse and vibrant tapestry of Vietnam. From its ancient dynasties to its modern economic boom, Vietnam has undergone a remarkable transformation that has captivated the imagination of travelers, historians, and adventurers alike.

Throughout this book, we have delved into the rich tapestry of Vietnam's history, exploring its ancient civilizations, colonial past, and tumultuous struggles for independence. We have traced the footsteps of emperors and revolutionaries, marveled at the architectural wonders of Hanoi and Hue, and reflected on the legacy of the Vietnam War, which left an indelible mark on the country and its people.

We have also ventured into the heart of Vietnamese culture, savoring the tantalizing flavors of its cuisine, marveling at the beauty of its art and architecture, and immersing ourselves in the rhythms of its music and dance. We have celebrated the diversity of its people, from the bustling streets of Ho Chi Minh City to the tranquil villages of the Mekong Delta, each contributing to the rich tapestry of Vietnamese society.

As we conclude our journey through Vietnam, it is clear that the country's story is far from over. With its thriving economy, dynamic culture, and strategic position in Southeast Asia, Vietnam is poised to play an increasingly important role on the global stage in the years to come.

But amidst the opportunities and challenges that lie ahead, one thing remains certain: the spirit of Vietnam - resilient, vibrant, and ever-changing - will continue to inspire and captivate all who are fortunate enough to experience its beauty and charm.

So as we bid farewell to this remarkable land, let us carry with us the memories and lessons learned from our journey through Vietnam, knowing that its story is far from finished, and that the best is yet to come.

Printed in Poland
by Amazon Fulfillment
Poland Sp. z o.o., Wrocław